D1616711

Great Eastern
Album

Liverpool Street station in the early years of the century. No. 1900 *Claud Hamilton* heads a down express, while beside it on station pilot duty is 0-4-4 tank No. 1110 carrying a Woolwich headboard.   [*L.P.C*

GREAT EASTERN
ALBUM

R. C. Riley

LONDON

IAN ALLAN LTD

First published 1968

Third impression 1975

7110 0063 8

© Ian Allan 1968

Published in the United Kingdom by Ian Allan Ltd, Shepperton, Surrey
and printed by Crampton & Sons Ltd, Sawston, Cambridge

INTRODUCTION

THE GREAT EASTERN line had a character all of its own. Whether at Liverpool Street to watch bustling steam suburban trains come and go with extraordinary frequency or travelling on some rural backwater in a coach that had seen better days, the character was there to be savoured and appreciated.

In fact the Great Eastern was a truly great railway. At grouping it ranked sixth in the country on a route mileage basis, while it led in the number of passengers carried. With the glamour of Pacific locomotives on the Scotch expresses there was a tendency to think of the Great Northern as the leading partner in the LNER group. This was not the case for the North Eastern Railway was the largest company and the Great Eastern came next. These two had an unusual feature in common—there were only three English counties where one railway company monopolised the traffic. The North Eastern enjoyed exclusive rights in Northumberland and Durham, while the Great Eastern had no opposition in Suffolk. Indeed apart from Cambridge and the London area the only rivalry encountered by the Great Eastern was that of the upstart Midland and Great Northern Joint Railway, a very second rate line in comparison.

The Great Eastern Railway in name originated in 1862 as a result of the amalgamation of the Eastern Counties, East Anglian, Eastern Union, East Suffolk, Newmarket and Norfolk Railways. The 1862 Act did no more than recognise a *fait accompli*, for the Eastern Counties Railway had already taken over the working of the other lines involved. By then most of the GE system that survives to-day was already in existence. First line to be opened had been that to Romford in 1839, extended by degrees to Colchester four years later. By 1845 it was possible to travel from London to Norwich, via Cambridge and Ely. The following year the line from Colchester to Ipswich was opened and by 1849 had been extended to Norwich. There were many branch lines still to be built. Places of special importance served subsequently include Cromer in 1877, Clacton in 1882 (Walton-on-the-Naze

Passengers about to board the Saturday 1.25 pm Enfield train at Liverpool Street, 22nd May, 1886.
[*Dr. R. F. Youell Collection*

had been reached by 1866) and Southend in 1889. An important development in 1882 was the opening of the GN & GE Joint Line from Huntingdon to Doncaster, via St. Ives, March, Spalding and Lincoln, which became a vital artery for south bound coal traffic between Doncaster and March. There were also joint working agreements on the Norfolk coast with the M & GN.

The Great Eastern had a rather splendid coat of arms. In the centre was the familiar cross and dagger of the City of London, flanked within an inscribed garter by the shields of Maldon, Ipswich, Norwich, Cambridge, Hertford, Northampton, Huntingdon and Middlesex. It was curious as much by its omissions as by those included; the GE only just penetrated Northamptonshire at Peterborough, 40 miles from the county town, a traditional LNWR stronghold. When in 1900 James Holden brought out the lovely " Claud Hamilton " 4-4-0s, they carried on their splashers a handsome cast iron plaque of the company's arms, individually painted in Stratford Works by girls from the Railway Orphanage. Incidentally, when the Eastern Counties locomotive works moved from Romford to Stratford in 1848 there was some outcry about such despoilation of a country district. The old ECR works still survived on the up side of the line at Gidea Park in the spring of 1968.

Even after it acquired that title the Great Eastern was not always a great railway. There was an unkind story of a ticket collector remonstrating with a youth of 16 for travelling at half price and being told that he had been only 12 when the train started! The turning point in Great Eastern affairs occurred in 1867 when Lord Cranborne was appointed Chairman. He later became Marquis of Salisbury and was destined to become Prime Minister. In four years he did much to restore confidence in the GER and to improve its solvency. When he left, the vacancy on the board was taken by a young man, Lord Claud Hamilton, who was to succeed to the chairmanship in 1893 and retain it until the end of the company's existence. A man with a meticulous attention for detail, he took great pains to know his staff and was much respected. In later years a man of substance in Suffolk passed the barrier at Liverpool Street to find Lord Claud Hamilton's saloon on the rear of his train. He accepted an invitation to join the Chairman and once under way ventured his opinion that the train was travelling faster than usual. Lord Claud Hamilton replied that he had heard of a charming new barmaid at Manningtree and he wished to see her. Sure enough an unscheduled stop was made, the great man paid a brief visit to the refreshment rooms, professed himself satisfied and returned to the train, which still reached Ipswich on time!

Holden J69 0-6-0 tank No. E.8619, normally Liverpool Street East Side Pilot, stands at North Woolwich on RCTS East London Rail Tour, 14th April 1951. From 1948 to 1953 this engine was in LNER green livery.   [R. C. Riley

Chairman from 1874 to 1893 was C. H. Parkes, who is commemorated to this day in Parkeston Quay, the railway port upstream from Harwich which was opened in 1883 and has an important and ever expanding continental traffic. The " ston " portion of the name was taken from Mr. Stone, the engineer responsible. Equally important, though, in Parkes' first year of office was the opening of Liverpool Street station. Many working class homes were demolished when this short extension was built at a cost of over £2,000,000. At first looked upon as a waste of money, within ten years it was inadequate for the traffic and with the opening of the East Side Suburban section in 1894 it reached its present size of 18 platforms. There is a sharp curve at the platform ends and then a 1 in 70 climb to Bethnal Green. More significant is the fact that there are only three pairs of running lines into the terminus and the amount of traffic handled at peak hours over these lines has to be seen to be believed.

By the end of the first world war the Liverpool Street suburban services had reached saturation point with 107,500,000 suburban passengers each year. Since 1914, with Lord Claud still in the chair, the GE had an American General Manager, H. W. Thornton, and he was given the task of improving the London area working. It was made difficult by the legacy of the GERs 1864 Act authorising the extension of suburban lines, which compelled it to carry workmen from Walthamstow to London at a return fare of 2d for a 17 mile journey. Later this concession was extended to Enfield, making it 21 miles for 2d. No other company carried its passengers so cheaply; indeed, in South London a 2d fare covered only eight miles. Hence the revenue brought in by suburban travellers could not possibly support the high cost of electrification.

Thornton set two of his best men to tackle the problem, F. V. Russell, Superintendent of Operation and H. F. Hilton, Assistant Superintendent, Southern Division. They studied every possible place where delays might occur and where conflicting movements could be avoided, whether at terminals or en route. Signalling and trackwork were improved and at Liverpool Street each platform on the West Side suburban section was provided with an engine dock so that after every departure the line could quickly be cleared for an incoming train. To assist passengers to find their coaches first class compartments had a distinctive yellow stripe and second class were blue—the term " jazz trains " applied at this time survived until the end of steam. The incredible result of the new timetable introduced in July 1920 was to increase the peak evening down service by 50% and the morning up service by no less than 75%.

This was the world's most intensive steam suburban service ever and it was largely handled by Holden's little 0-6-0 tanks designed for shunting work, their 4ft 0in wheels turning merrily at anything up to 60 mph. Of course the 2-4-2 tanks and 0-4-4 tanks played their part, but best remembered were the little six-coupled tanks, nicknamed " Buckjumpers ". Why the name? The GE was a Westinghouse brake line and with full loads and short stops steam was kept on right to the platform

Spartan comfort provided by the six-a-side suburban trains of 1899. [*British Railways*

end, where a sharp brake application brought the train to rest in the right place. Starting away, the driver fully opened the regulator at once and the engine gave a visible jump as it got under way, acceleration being quite rapid. In 1915 Hill built two 0-6-2 tanks for suburban services, but the class was not multiplied until 1921 when ten more appeared, followed by another ten just after grouping, the last engines built at Stratford. The LNER later added another 112 to the class.

My first experience of a Great Eastern suburban train came on a visit to Stratford in 1935. The GE stock in use had ¾ height partitions between compartments, so economising in lights and making it possible to see the length of the carriage. As we left Liverpool Street the tortured notes of a badly played violin came from the next compartment giving a barely recognisable rendering of " Red Sails in the Sunset ". On the approach to Bethnal Green a grubby cap with coins in it was thrust over the partition. The station stop was brief but it enabled the itinerant musician to move up a few compartments and the process was repeated at Coborn Road and Stratford. This was a regular feature of suburban travel from Liverpool Street, perhaps not inappropriate for the Jazz Trains!

Reverting to the Holden 0-6-0 tanks, one of the last acts of the LNER prior to nationalisation was to paint in passenger livery pilot engines at certain important stations since they were much in the public eye. As a result some hitherto obscure tank engines attained a degree of fame almost overnight and none more so than Liverpool Street's East Side Pilot, J69 0-6-0 tank No. 8619, so repainted in January 1948. It may have provided the idea for a drawing in *Punch* depicting the disgruntled crew of a brand new diesel ignored by passengers who stood admiring the small tank engine that brought in the empty coaches. The BTC, perhaps less sensitive than its successor, did not mind a joke against itself and used the drawing on its Christmas card! The East Side Pilot reverted to black five years later and then in 1959 reappeared in Great Eastern blue. Whatever its livery, it was always immaculately turned out, as indeed is its present day diesel replacement.

The smart and unique blue livery of the Great Eastern originated in 1882 on the occasion of the public opening of Epping Forest by Queen Victoria. The engine of the Royal Train to Chingford was specially painted Royal Blue, and this livery was adopted as standard for passenger engines until rigid economies enforced during the 1914 war brought an end to it. The Great Eastern's association with royalty was of long standing. In 1861 the Sandringham estate was acquired for the Prince of Wales, later King Edward VII, and the following year the branch from Kings Lynn to Hunstanton was opened, with its attractive station at Wolferton for the royal traffic. Until the advent of the Claud Hamilton 4-4-0s, Royal Trains were often worked by T19 2-4-0s, which continued to provide motive power to and from Wolferton for some time, since reversal at Kings Lynn was necessary. The first engines earmarked for royal duties were Clauds specially finished for this purpose. In LNER days Super Clauds 8783 and 8787 were chosen and together with *Claud Hamilton* were the only members of the class in green passenger livery until wartime austerity ended that, although the Royal Clauds reappeared briefly in green after the war. By then their royal activities were largely confined to the Hunstanton branch, their main line duties having been taken over by " Sandringham 4-6-0 No. 1671 *Royal Sovereign*. The Hunstanton branch, long operated by diesel units went over to conductor guard working in 1967, and Wolferton became an unstaffed halt. The service was withdrawn in 1969. The station buildings have since been auctioned as three separate dwelling houses. A few of the ornate golden crowned lamps with lion and unicorn crests survive on what is now private land, the remainder having been sold.

Since the royal family has always taken a great interest in horse racing it is appropriate to recall another form of special traffic handled by the Great Eastern, that in connection with Newmarket races. The first railway to Newmarket was from Great Chesterford, opened in 1848, but it became insolvent and the section between Great Chesterford and Six Mile Bottom was closed in 1851, in which year the direct line to Cambridge was opened. Three years later the line was extended from Newmarket to Bury St. Edmunds, and its Act stipulated that the amenities of Newmarket Heath must be preserved. In consequence the line threads an 1,100 yd. single line tunnel, the longest on the GER, on which six of its only nine tunnels were in the London area. For many years Bury trains had to shunt out of the old terminus and then resume their journey, but this practice ceased in 1902 when the present station was opened. Architecturally among the finest of many well designed station buildings

Two horse power at Woodbridge on the East Suffolk line, October 1956. Until its closure horses used to work the Woodbridge Tramway as far as Melton. [*R. C. Riley*

in East Anglia, the old Newmarket station still survives, although in poor condition. It was an appropriate place for the last shunting horse on British Railways to be employed. "Charlie", transferred from Diss a few years earlier, was honourably retired in 1967. Newmarket horse box specials took Great Eastern engines as far afield as Nottingham, while from 1930 onwards the LNER allowed Gresley Pacifics to work race specials between Kings Cross and Newmarket, the first of their type to use Great Eastern metals. It was not until British Railways' days and the introduction of the "Britannias" that Pacific locomotives began regular working on the GE line.

Indeed, with one notable exception, Great Eastern engines were on the small side but nevertheless strong and capable machines. It was fortunate in being served by a long line of distinguished locomotive engineers. First of these on formation of the GER was Robert Sinclair who went to the Eastern Counties Railway from the Caledonian in 1856. He introduced a measure of standardisation and one class of mixed traffic 2-4-0s numbered no less than 110 engines. In 1866 Samuel Johnson took over and found new engines so urgently needed, that five 2-4-0s under construction for the North British Railway were diverted to the GE. Forty engines of a similar design were built between 1867 and 1872, and since most of them came from Sharp Stewart they were known as the "Little Sharpies". They did excellent work and the last survived until 1913. Johnson also built two classes of 0-6-0 freight engine, totalling 110 in all, but these were withdrawn by 1902. This is the more remarkable because Johnson went to the Midland Railway in 1873 on which line 865 0-6-0 goods engines were built to his design, none being withdrawn until 1925 while three of the earliest survived until 1964.

Johnson's successor, William Adams, came from the North London Railway but later became better known on the LSWR. Like Johnson he built 0-4-4 tanks for passenger work and 0-4-2 tanks

9

for branch trains. His 4-4-0 " Ironclads " intended for passenger work proved unsuitable and were relegated to freight trains. The only notweorthy feature of his freight engine design was that it was the first 2-6-0 to run in this country and the only example built by the GER. At least two of these engines carried the name MOGUL on the combined splasher and sandbox, so providing a class name for subsequent generations of the type. This was their only claim to fame—they steamed so badly that they could not haul the loads taken by smaller engines and they were very uneconomical; within eight years the class was extinct. Massey Bromley succeeded Adams but held the reins only from 1878 to 1881. He produced some short lived single drivers, 70 workmanlike 0-4-4 tanks, some 0-6-0 ballast engines and 0-6-0 tanks. T. W. Worsdell then had four years at Stratford before going to the NER. His passenger tender engines were not conspicuously successful, but he left his mark in several ways, not least in the blue livery. His 2-4-2 tanks were called " Gobblers " because of their high coal consumption but a modified design was successful and long lived. His 0-6-0s, best known as the J.15s in later years, were so useful that nearly 300 were built between 1883 and 1913, the 272 which survived at grouping forming the largest single class of engine to come into LNER ownership. Finally he designed the curious little tram engines, once a familiar sight on the Wisbech & Upwell Tramway and on quayside lines at such places as Ipswich and Yarmouth.

Including two temporarily in office the Great Eastern had now had seven locomotive engineers in just over 20 years, but there was to be at last a long period of continuity. James Holden, in command from 1885 to 1907, was succeeded by his son, S. D. Holden, in turn succeeded five years later by A. J. Hill, in office until the grouping. James Holden came from Swindon—need one say more? Apart from his locomotives he was responsible for some fine carriages. During his 22 years in office nearly 900 engines of his own design were built at Stratford in addition to more than 200 of Worsdell's design. With improvements in sanding, the single driver had a renewed vogue as an express engine in the latter years of the 19th Century. Holden designed two such types, both successful with light loads, but as trains were becoming heavier his singles were short lived. His express and mixed traffic 2-4-0s did much better; the last survivor of the latter engines and one of his admirable 0-6-0 tanks already mentioned are to be seen in Clapham Museum.

Stratford, no longer the country district it had been in 1848, had an extensive oil gas plant where gas for carriage lighting was produced, but the oil residue was fouling the Lea and Channelsea rivers and bringing justifiable complaints from the authorities. It was in the early eighties that the solution was found and plans drawn up by Joshua Phillips, Chief Chemist of the GER for oil burning locomotives to consume the waste oil. The first engine so fitted was Holden's express 2-4-0 No. 760 named *Petrolea* in honour of the event, and eventually about 60 engines of various classes were fitted including some " Claud Hamilton " 4-4-0s. Holden's masterpiece, the prototype engine having been built in 1900. The scheme went well for some years but was discontinued because the waste oil eventually proved insufficient and imported oil was considerably more costly than home produced coal.

A pioneer in the use of motor omnibuses in 1904, the GE actually built 12 such vehicles at Stratford Works. The rigidity of the springs made these vehicles rather fallible. Two of them are seen on Lowestoft duties about 1905.

[B.T.C. Curator of Historical Relics

Motive power contrast—Holden's 80 ton Decapod dwarfs 1876 Neilson saddle tank No. 229. The latter was sold in 1918 and still survives at Chepstow. *[W. O. Skeat Collection*

Holden's final fling was no more than an experiment, but a successful one. In 1901 the GER monopoly of the North Eastern London suburban traffic was threatened by schemes for electric railways, the promoters of which claimed an acceleration unattainable by steam. Holden was set the task of building a steam engine that could reach 30 mph within 30 seconds from a stand with a 300 tons load. The Holden 0-6-0 tanks with 15 four-wheelers, about 240 tons fully loaded, attained 20 mph within 30 seconds. Holden's solution was the formidable and revolutionary Decapod, a ten-coupled three cylinder tank engine weighing 80 tons, concentrated on a wheelbase of less than 20 feet. After some initial difficulties were overcome the Decapod was successfully proven—it attained 30 mph in under 30 seconds with a 355 tons load. The GER won its case, the electric railway bill was defeated in parliament, and the Decapod was converted to an 0-8-0 freight engine, being both too heavy and more powerful than necessary for existing requirements, apart from which it was an unsteady riding machine.

Holden junior had only four years in command but in that time he produced the famous " 1500 " Class 4-6-0s. These were the logical developments of the Clauds, which had been progressively modified, and had reached a total of 111 engines in 1911 when the first 4-6-0 appeared. Like all GE engines, the Decapod in both forms and a few four-coupled tanks and the six-coupled tram engines excepted, the " 1500s " were inside cylinder engines. No. 1506 had a working life of less than four months, being damaged beyond repair in an accident at Colchester in 1913. By 1921 there were 70 of these useful 4-6-0s and ten more were built in 1928. In 1922 one of the Clauds was rebuilt with a larger diameter boiler and others followed while ten new " Super Clauds " were built in 1923. In LNER days many of the Clauds and " 1500s " were rebuilt with improved front end and round topped firebox in accordance with Gresley's standards. Several unrebuilt " 1500s " found a new sphere of usefulness on the former Great North of Scotland Railway. During the 1939-45 war, because of their high route availability, rebuilt " 1500s " hauled Ambulance Trains all over the South and West of England, appearing on such unlikely lines as the Somerset & Dorset, the Thame branch to Oxford and thence to Worcester and Hereford. Even allocation of LNER " Sandringham " 4-6-0s to the GE from 1928 onwards had not removed them from top express work and eventually the last " 1500 " outlived the newer engines.

At the 1923 grouping the GER owned 1336 engines on capital stock and seven departmental engines, and with few exceptions these were to be very long lived—indeed 773 of them came into British Railways' ownership. There were no radical changes, therefore, in LNER days. Certain GE types found new homes on other sections, notably the Holden 0-6-0 tanks, while as early as 1923 some GNR 2-6-0s were transferred to the GE and other classes followed in small numbers. The large Hill J.20 0-6-0s were displaced to some extent by Gresley 2-8-0s but it was not until the 1930s that bridges were strengthened for these large engines to work London bound freight traffic. The line to Shenfield was electrified in 1949—then a motive power transformation really started with the appearance of the first main line diesel in 1957. Even so, and despite the arrival on the scene of diesel multiple units for branch work there still survived a number of J.15 0-6-0s on such duties, their tall chimneys making them look older than they really were. They even had their moments of glory—in 1948 one had come to the rescue of an ailing B.1 4-6-0 at Chelmsford and steamed proudly into Liverpool Street complete with The East Anglian headboard!

The old order changes—" Britannia " No. 70009 *Alfred the Great* enters Stowmarket with the 1.30 pm Liverpool Street-Norwich, August 1956.   Rebuilt " Claud " 4-4-0 No. 62605 waits to work the connecting train to Bury St. Edmunds.   [*Dr. Ian C. Allen*

Until the end of the 19th Century there were few fast schedules worthy of note, but it has to be remembered that with many adverse gradients and speed restrictions on its route the GE was not an easy line to work.   In 1897 with the provision of water troughs at Ipswich and Tivetshall it was possible to run the Cromer Express non-stop from Liverpool Street to North Walsham, 130 miles in 158 minutes.   Some spectacular accelerations were introduced in 1914 but wartime conditions soon compelled easier schedules.   In 1937 the " East Anglian " was introduced, a very light train which ran the 115 miles to Norwich in 130 minutes, including an Ipswich stop, but this was far below the work of the Clauds in GE days with the heavy " Norfolk Coast Express ".   It took some time to recover from the Second World War and it was not until 1951 that outstanding improvements were made to the GE timetable.   By then the BR " Britannia " 4-6-2s were replacing Thomson B.1 4-6-0s, although until the " Britannias " reached sufficient numbers some SR Pacifics were loaned.   The Pacifics were so diagrammed to do the round trip between London and Norwich twice each day and the pre-war " East Anglian " schedule with 220 tons was now equalled with 410 tons.

In the autumn of 1952 the down " Broadsman " was accelerated to a two hour schedule, inclusive of an Ipswich stop.   Since then with progressive accelerations there has been some remarkable locomotive performance on the GE line.   To-day the motive power may be more predictable and aesthetically less satisfying but the Great Eastern continues to be efficiently run and retains much of its character.

In compiling Great Eastern Album I have been fortunate in having the ready assistance of many friends and in particular Dr. Ian C. Allen and John Watling.   Among others who kindly placed their collections at my disposal were Dr. W. J. Naunton, Dr. R. F. Youell and Messrs. J. A. Gardner, G. H. Pember, W. O. Skeat, J. L. Smith and B. D. J. Walsh.   The F. J. Agar pictures appear by courtesy of Pamlin Prints, those of the late W. H. C. Kelland by courtesy of the Bournemouth Railway Club and those of the late K. A. C. R. Nunn are the copyright of the Locomotive Club of Great Britain, whose plans to publish them will interest all GE enthusiasts.   I am only sorry that Ken Nunn himself was not here to advise me—his great readiness to help and encyclopaedic knowledge of GE matters are sadly missed.   The late H. F. Hilton's pictures appear by courtesy of R. Hilton and British Railways Eastern Region Press Office.   In making my selection I have endeavoured to choose photographs that are complimentary to those in " THE GREAT EASTERN RAILWAY " by Cecil J. Allen, now in its fifth edition.

LIVERPOOL STREET

Holden's oil burning 2-2-2 No. 1008 stands in Liverpool Street with the Cromer Express, which from July 1896 ran the 131 miles to North Walsham non-stop. A preliminary trial was staged in November 1895 which ran through to Cromer without stopping, a journey of 138 miles and no chance of taking water en route. Water troughs were installed before the regular service began. Holden's 2-2-2s, built 1889-93, survived only until 1907. [B. D. J. Walsh collection

The original station in 1909 with " Claud Hamilton " class 4-4-0 No. 1858 off a
main line arrival.
[L. Ward Collection

LIVERPOOL STREET

East Side Suburban station opened in 1894.   Platform 14 carries a notice showing
that it was used for New Cross and Croydon trains.   After 1911 trains ceased to run
south of New Cross and the service was withdrawn two years later on electrification
of the East London line.
[J. L. Smith Collection

Peak hour scene at the top of Bethnal Green bank—mostly suburban trains visible but in the distance is a rebuilt " Humpty Dumpty " 2-4-0 on a down express.

[L.P C

BETHNAL GREEN

Bethnal Green station soon after 1900 with a Holden 0-6-0 tank leaving on a train from Chingford. [L.P.C.

Fenchurch Street started life in 1841 as the city terminus of the London and Blackwall Railway which was leased and operated by the GER from 1866. In 1854 the London, Tilbury & Southend line opened and although originally connected with the Eastern Counties Railway it obtained its independence in 1862 although worked by GE engines and stock until 1880. At left an LTSR train enters headed by a 4-4-2 tank, about 1910. At right two GE tanks used on services to Ongar, Ilford and Woolwich. GE line trains ceased to use Fenchurch Street when the Shenfield line was electrified in 1949.   [L.P.C.

FENCHURCH STREET

Holden's smallest 0-6-0 tanks were 20 engines of 1888-93 which formed LNER Class J65. Several ran on the Fenchurch Street-Blackwall service as 2-4-0 tanks with the front section of the coupling rod removed. In this condition was No. 155 pausing at Stepney East with a train from Blackwall. This service ceased in 1926.
[J. L. Smith Collection

Wood Street, Walthamstow about 1900 with two Holden 0-6-0 tanks in the shed yard.
[*H. F. Hilton*

LONDON SUBURBAN

Ilford carriage sidings in May 1911. The electric car sheds now occupy this site.
[*British Railways*

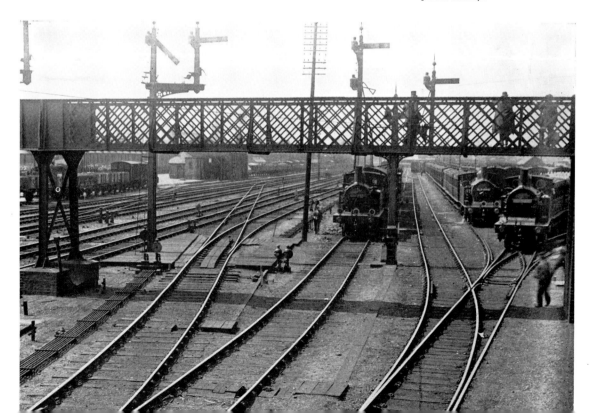

ESSEX STATIONS

ABOVE: The busy scene at Marks Tey about 1900. An oil burning 2-4-0 heads a down main line train, while an early 0-4-4 tank waits with a train from the Haverhill branch. In the foreground a Worsdell 0-6-0 shunts a pick up goods train.   [*H. F. Hilton*

No. 097, last survivor of Massey Bromley's 0-4-4 tanks enters Saffron Walden with a freight from Audley End, December 1910.   [*British Railways*

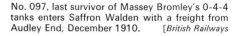

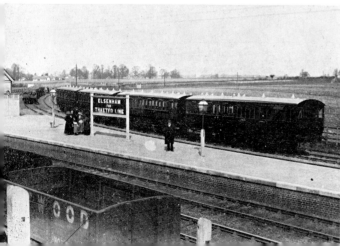

Elsenham station in 1913 showing the Thaxted branch platform. In the siding are the 1891-2 coaches then recently converted for use on the branch, with centre gangways and end doors.
[*British Railways*

THE MARITIME SCENE

TSS " Copenhagen " at Parkeston Quay awaiting arrival of the 8.30 pm continental express, November 30th, 1912.   Built in 1907 the " Copenhagen was " sunk by enemy action in the North Sea, March 1917.

[*C. D. E. Roper Nunn, courtesy Dr. R. F. Youell*

19

A Worsdell 0-6-0 shunts the goods yard at Bury St. Edmunds about 1900.   In the background is the impressive station building.   [H. F. Hilton

EAST ANGLIA

Wisbech station and engine shed about 1900.   At right tramway type coaches used on the Upwell line.   The total stock consisted of eight four-wheeled coaches built in 1884 and 1890 and two bogie coaches of 1884.   A Guards Van converted from an 1875 3rd Brake was added in 1903.   [British Railways

The 1.30 pm train to Yarmouth Vauxhall leaves Norwich Thorpe, 15th April, 1911, headed by *Little Sharpie* 2-4-0 No. 28, built in 1868 and among the last survivors.

[*K A. C. R. Nunn*

NORFOLK

Holden 4-2-2 No. 14 seen leaving Norwich Thorpe about 1903 was a very short lived engine. Built in 1898 it was withdrawn nine years later.   [*H. F. Hilton*

CROMER EXPRESS

Cromer station about 1905 with " Claud Hamilton " 4-4-0 No. 1897 and at right a
T19 Class 2-4-0.   [*L.P.C.*

2-4-0

TYPES

One of the long lived "Intermediate" 2-4-0s (LNER Class E4) leaving Clacton. The line from Thorpe-le-Soken to Clacton was not doubled until 1941.
[*J. L. Smith collection*

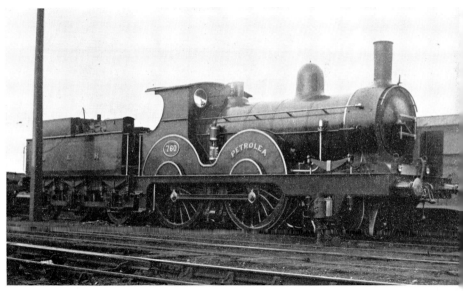

No. 760 *Petrolea,* one of 110 express 2-4-0s of the T19 Class built by Holden between 1886 and 1897. This engine was adapted for oil burning in 1893 and carried 500 gallons of oil fuel in a rectangular tank on the tender.
[*L. & G.R.P.*

Another T19, coal burning engine No. 1038, built in 1897. This engine was one of 29 scrapped in original condition between 1908 and 1913. [*Dr. W. J. Naunton Collection*

Between 1902 and 1904, 21 of the remaining T19s were rebuilt with a large boiler and Belpaire firebox. They looked top heavy and were nicknamed "Humpty Dumpties". They were too heavy at the front end to permit the additional weight of superheating tubes and all were withdrawn between 1913 and 1920. No. 1014 was recorded at Cambridge in 1913.
[W. H. C. Kelland

REBUILT 2-4-0

Rebuilt 2-4-0 No. 770 heads the 10.25 am through express from York to Liverpool Street into the terminus, 7th May, 1909. This through service was in operation from 1892 to 1914 and for several years GE engines were allocated to York. Another important passenger service over the GN & GE Joint Line was the North Country Continental between Harwich and Doncaster introduced in 1883. [K. A. C. R. Nunn

The 60 surviving T19 2-4-0s were rebuilt to 4-4-0 between 1905 and 1908 and apart from the use of bogies were similar to the " Humpty Dumpties ". From 1913 most of them were superheated, but two were withdrawn as early as 1922. The superheating transformed the performance of these engines No. 741 in wartime livery heads an up parcels train through Gidea Park.   [L. & G.R.P.

REBUILT 4-4-0

Gidea Park station was opened in December 1910 as a four track station, but the line thence from Romford was not quadrupled until 1931. Three light engines run through the station, No. 735, rebuilt from a T19 2-4-0, and two " Claud Hamilton " 4-4-0s.   [L. & G.R.P.

No. 1804, built in 1910, heads a train of miscellaneous stock through Seven Kings in pre-war days.

[*A. G. Ellis Collection*

CLAUD HAMILTON 4-4-0

An earlier engine, No. 1881, built in 1901, heads a down express through Brentwood.

[*G. H. Pember Collection*

One of the earlier engines, No. 1508, heads an up Pullman Car express south of Cambridge in 1913.

[*W. H. C. Kelland*

HOLDEN 4-6-0

No. 1541 was the first of 20 engines built by Wm. Beardmore of Glasgow in 1920-1.   Although in wartime grey livery the finish and lining was more elaborate than usual at this period.   Also in 1920 Beardmore's overhauled six " Claud Hamilton " 4-4-0s at their works.   [*J. L. Smith Collection*

DECAPOD

ABOVE: In rebuilt form as an 0-8-0, No. 20 stands on the 9.20 pm empties to March at Temple Mills sidings, November 1912. It was withdrawn the following year.   [*C. D. E. Roper Nunn   courtesy Dr. R. F. Youell*

RIGHT: Rear view of Holden's impressive ten-coupled engine.   Built in 1902 it was purely experimental and was converted to an eight-coupled tender engine for freight work four years later.
[*W. O. Skeat Collection*

Small Holden tank No. 153 as a 2-4-0 stands at Bishops Stortford. *[L. & G.R.P.*

SIX COUPLED TANKS

Holden 0-6-0 tank No. 335, built in 1890 and finished in blue passenger livery, stands at Enfield Town. *[L.P.C.*

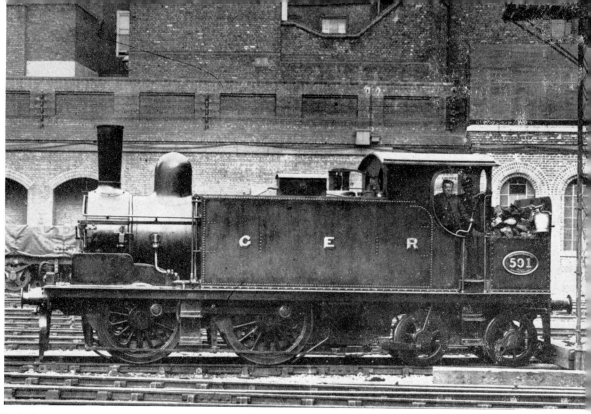

Typical example of earlier suburban engines was this Massey Bromley 0-4-4 tank.
The last into service of 60 built between 1878 and 1883, No. 591 stands outside
Liverpool Street. These engines were withdrawn between 1904 and 1912.

[C. R. L. Coles Collection

FOUR
COUPLED
TANKS

Last word in GE 2-4-2 tanks were 20 engines built by S. D. Holden in 1911-12.
These had very roomy cabs and as LNER Class F6 remained in the London area until
the Shenfield electrification in 1949. No. 9 was recorded at Stratford.

[J. L. Smith Collection

2-4-2 Tank No. 242 passes Gidea Park with a down Brentwood local composed of a mixture of five and six-a-side four-wheelers (LNER Class F4).   [L. & G.R.P.

FOUR COUPLED TANKS

No. 1075 pauses at Gidea Park with a down local.   These were the largest GE 2-4-2 tanks.   Built between 1893 and 1902 they were a tank version of the " Intermediate " 2-4-0s.   (LNER Class F3.)   [L. & G.R.P.

After Worsdell produced his very satisfactory Y14 0-6-0 (LNER Class J15) in 1882, he produced a variation in 1893 which had cylinders of the T19 2-4-0 type with underhung valve chests. The boiler needed to be pitched higher but was no larger. 81 engines were built to this design but they were sluggish and steamed badly. All were withdrawn by 1925. No. 0545 was recorded at Cambridge in 1913. (LNER Class J14.)

[W. H. C. Kelland

No. 1151, one of Holden's 0-6-0 goods engines which appeared in 1900 and had the same boiler as that used on *Claud Hamilton*. In 1902 Holden tried a Belpaire firebox on No. 1189 and all were eventually so rebuilt. 46 round topped boiler engines came into LNER hands as Class J16, the last being rebuilt in 1932.

[J. L. Smith Collection

No. 1240, at Cambridge in 1914, was the first of ten S. D. Holden 0-6-0s built two years earlier and notable for the concidorablo front end overhang. (LNER Class J18.)

[W. H. C. Kelland

No. 844, an 1889 built engine, heads an up freight at Gidea Park. As LNER Class J15 the last of the class was not withdrawn until 1962. No. 930 of this type was fully erected at Stratford in 1891 in ten hours, a record that has never been equalled.   [*L. & G.R.P.*

No. 1214, Belpaire version of J. Holden's 0-6-0 opposite, was recorded at Cambridge in 1914. (LNER Class J17.) [*W. H. C Kelland*

FREIGHT
ENGINES

No. 1282, one of the large Hill goods engines built in 1922. (LNER Class J20.) These engines proved particularly useful on the heavy coal trains which were always such a prominent feature of the GN & GE Joint Line between Doncaster and March.
                   [*Real Photographs Ltd.*

Stratford Works shunter A was a standard Manning Wardle H Class 0-4-0 saddle tank built for the GER in December 1872. It was originally No. 200 and was said at one time to have been named *The Chairman* although name and number were removed when it became Works engine A in 1895. It lasted until 1921.
[*R. C. Riley Collection*

SMALL TANK ENGINES

Stratford Works shunter D was one of five 0-6-0 tanks built by Ruston & Proctor, Lincoln, in 1868. Three of them, Nos. 204-6, had cranes fitted 1891-3 and were very long lived, being withdrawn between 1950 and 1952.
[*J. L. Smith Collection*

One of the Neilson 0-4-0 saddle tanks, No. 231 of 1903, carried sideplates and cowcatchers similar to the tram engines. Stationed at Colchester, No. 231 worked on quayside lines at Hythe until withdrawal in 1931.
[*J. L. Smith Collection*

Four-coupled tram engine No. 131 hauls an Upwell train along Elm Road, Wisbech. Built in 1884 this engine was the first of the class withdrawn, in 1907. The presence of the guard's brake proves this photograph to have been taken after 1903. [*Dr. W. J. Naunton Collection*

TRAM ENGINES

Four-coupled tram engine No. 132 at Upwell, March 1923, with bogie tram coach No. 7, which was withdrawn in 1951 and sold to a film company for use in " The Titfield Thunderbolt ". [*W. Potter*

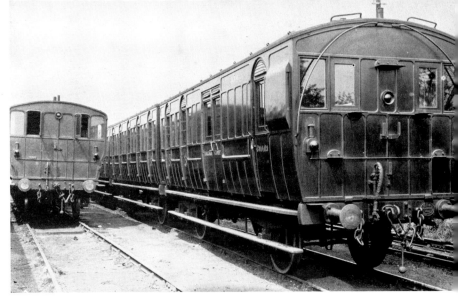

Four-wheeled suburban coaches. The set at left was of the five-a-side type built from 1872 and too old to be widened to six-a-side after 1900. The set at right was the first built new to accommodate six-a-side. Built in 1899 it was the only such set to have wooden underframes, all subsequent coaches having steel underframes. Many but not all of these coaches were converted to bogie vehicles between 1914 and 1923. Note the end lamps, which were gas lit.

[D. A. Ives Collection

ROLLING STOCK

A revolution in GE suburban stock occurred in 1900 with the first bogie train for such services. It consisted of a six compartment 8-wheeled 3rd Brake at either end of six 12-wheeled coaches, one of which was an eight compartment 1st. This set seated 808 passengers and was used for many years on the Enfield line, although by the 1930s it was on the Ilford services. it ended its days on the North Woolwich line, although not as a complete set, being withdrawn in 1948. It is here seen leaving Ipswich on a Saturday relief Liverpool Street-Yarmouth train in July 1939.

[Dr. Ian C. Allen

A typical GE Full Brake, No. 553 built in 1890. This vehicle is being carefully restored at Lowestoft by the GER Group, a select body of four dedicated enthusiasts who have achieved much in the preservation of relics and records. A similar 1885 vehicle is owned by the West Midlands RPS at Hednesford. Much still had to be done when this photograph was taken in 1967.

[J. Watling

THE
LNER
SCENE

Pride of the line, one of S. D. Holden's magnificent 1500 Class 4-6-0s heads an up express near Shenfield, 15th August, 1925. By this time only the livery had changed —the scene is pure GER in all other respects and the line was to retain most of its old characteristics for many years. The signal retains a Coligny-Welch distant signal distinguishing lamp. The lamp was patented by Welch in 1898, Coligny financing its production. It was adopted from 1906 by the three Southern companies and the GER. At this time distant signals showed red or green aspects at night and the fishtail lamp was a useful means of identifying a distant signal, avoiding the use of a third colour. From 1925 the yellow aspect replaced the red and the Coligny-Welch lamp was discarded.

[F. J. Agar

37

STATIONS

ABOVE: Maldon East, Eastern Counties Railway built 1848. A fine brick building in Jacobean style with stone detailing, a worthy station for this ancient borough whose coat of arms found a place in the GER armorial device. The passenger service was withdrawn in 1964.

[H. G. Lawlor

LEFT: Somerleyton, built by the Lowestoft Harbour & Railway Company in 1847 and leased to the Norfolk Railway. It was built in the style of nearby Somerleyton Hall built at the same period. On the Norwich-Lowestoft line, the station is now unstaffed. [J. Watling

BELOW: The austerity of Manea provides a contrast to those above. Also dating to 1847, it is situated on the ECR line from Ely to March. The all wooden construction used in the Fens allowed for the possibility of extensive ground settlement, while withstanding the vibration of passing trains, which is excessive in such conditions. Coldham and Stonea were similar. [J. Watling

ABOVE: The second station at Wolferton, built in 1895 and used for Royal journeys to and from Sandringham. [B.R.

RIGHT: Halesworth station on the East Suffolk line is not outstanding architecturally and part of the station house was destroyed by enemy action about 1940. When the platforms were lengthened in 1922 it was necessary to provide a movable portion where a road was crossed. "Super Claud" No. 8852 approaches with an up Yarmouth express, 28th July, 1934. [S. W. Baker

BELOW: Opening the Halesworth movable platform to road traffic after passage of a train, October 1956. [R. C. Riley

STRATFORD

ABOVE: Stratford was not only the largest engine shed on the GER but also on the whole of British Railways with an allocation of over 400 engines, of which 100 were out at sub-sheds. In this view in GER days Worsdell 0-6-0s predominate, with tank engines in the background.

[L.P.C.

RIGHT: In the foreground a relic of James Holden's oil burning era—an oil fuel crane on the former " Oil Road ", with the modern coaling plant in the background, August 30th, 1958. [J. A Gardner

The B17 Class 4-6-0s were designed by Gresley for the Great Eastern Section. 1928 pioneer of the class, No. 2800 *Sandringham*, stands at Stratford specially groomed to work the " Eastern Belle ". In the distance above the tender can be seen the oil fuel tanks that once served the " Oil Road ". Oil firing was resumed during the 1921 and 1926 coal strikes.   [*Dr. R. F. Youell Collection*

41

In near original condition, No. 1900 *Claud Hamilton* as first repainted in LNER livery in 1923. It was later renumbered 8900. All GE engines had 7000 added to their original numbers by the LNER and this system prevailed until the 1946 renumbering scheme.

[*Dr. R. F. Youell Collection*

CLAUD HAMILTON 4-4-0

No. 8820, then one of the few unsuperheated engines, heads an Ipswich train out of Cambridge, 1931.

[*Dr. Ian C. Allen*

No. 8885 was unusual in having had the decorative footplating removed in 1931, the only other unrebuilt Claud so treated being No. 8896 three years later, the latter engine surviving in this form as No. 62507 in BR days. No. 8885 was in charge of a down express near Harold Wood, 18th August, 1932. The bridge in the background was in course of demolition in readiness for the widening to four tracks of the line between Romford and Shenfield, completed at the end of 1933.   [E. R. Wethersett

In final unrebuilt form, No. 8887 heads a down main line stopping train out of Romford. The GNR type chimney was first used on a " Claud " in 1930, but from 1936 about 40 engines were so fitted.
                    [J. G. Dewing

No. 8813, rebuilt in 1926, approaches Colchester with an up Clacton train, 4th August, 1933. [*F. J. Agar*

SUPER CLAUDS

No. 8800, a 1927 rebuild, heads the "Eastern Belle" pullman excursion through Chadwell Heath, 30th May, 1933.   Use of pullman cars on GE trains had not been an unqualified success.   In LNER days they were first confined to Newmarket race specials and then used on the "Eastern Belle", which ran to Clacton, Cromer, Yarmouth and other coastal resorts.   [*E. R. Wethersett*

44

No. 8792 was rebuilt in 1928 and in the mid-thirties was often used as Kings Lynn's Royal Engine on the Hunstanton branch. Hence its well groomed appearance as it leaves March with a Kings Lynn-Ely train. *[J. G. Dewing*

With its later number, No. 2590 leaves the Framlingham branch at Wickham Market junction with an excursion to Felixstowe, July 1947. This was the last survivor of four " Super Clauds " to come into BR hands and it was withdrawn in 1952. *[Dr. Ian C. Allen*

ROYAL CLAUDS

No. 8783 heads the Royal Train from Kings Cross to Wolferton through Cambridge, May 1938. Liverpool Street was not normally used for Royal traffic because of the formalities needed for Royalty entering the City of London. In LNER days and after, Kings Cross was used; before grouping such trains used St. Pancras by means of running powers over the Midland Railway.

[R. F. Roberts

Portrait of No. 8787 at Peterborough East showing the normal daily condition of the two Royal engines. No. 8783 was fitted with a copper capped chimney to add to the effect.

[T. G. Hepburn

REBUILT CLAUDS

Commencing with No. 8848 in January 1933, an eventual total of 105 " Clauds " were rebuilt with round-topped firebox and a larger boiler of the same diameter as that of the " Super Clauds ". No. 8875 leaves Ipswich with a Felixstowe excursion, the GE 1900 built bogie suburban train providing spartan comfort for its patrons. [J. G. Dewing

No. 8885 stands at Sudbury with a Cambridge - Colchester train, 1946, showing wartime livery style with NE lettering on the tender. [G. W. Powell

Rebuilt " Clauds " put up some spirited performances on the tightly timed Southend line trains. No. 8900 Claud Hamilton passes Chadwell Heath with the 2.0 pm Liverpool Street-Southend, 31st May, 1933. This was the second of the class to be rebuilt, in February 1933. It was an early withdrawal, in 1947, when its nameplates were transferred to another of the class. [E. R. Wethersett

HOLDEN
4-6-0s

No. 8542 stands at Ipswich with a down stopping train. This engine was disfigured by the fitting of an A.C.F.I. Feed-water heater, in common with most of the unrebuilt engines in pre-war days. [*W. H. C. Kelland*

No. 8579, one of ten built in 1928 by Beyer Peacock, was recorded on an up Marylebone express at Nottingham Victoria, on which it was running in between Manchester and Leicester. Four years later this was the first engine to be rebuilt with a round topped firebox as Class B12/3. [*T. G. Hepburn*

No. 8541 pulls out of Yarmouth South Town with an up express in the summer of 1937. *[G. W. Powel*

Typical of the period was this up Cambridge slow train at Littlebury, 27th July, 1934, with an extraordinary variety of coaching stock. No. 8572, as BR No. 61572, was the last of the class withdrawn in 1961, and was sold to the M&GN Preservation Society. *[E. R. Wethersett*

REBUILT
4-6-0s

Among the last two survivors was No. 8023 standing in the sidings at Ely with stock for a Cambridge local.   This engine and No. 8039 lasted until 1944.

[J. G. Dewing

D13 CLASS 4-4-0

No. 8037 heads a Stour Valley line train near Stapleford, 1st July 1932.

[E. R. Wethersett

No. 7416, in original condition with stovepipe chimney, passes Cromer Junction with a Norwich-Cromer train.   Like the GE London area, Norwich area trains had a special route indicating headcode.   The calling-on signal visible just above the dome was used when Cromer and Sheringham trains were combined at this point.   *[T. G. Hepburn*

E4 CLASS 2-4-0

No. 7453 pulls out of Norwich with a Lowestoft train.   Note that it has a tender of the type formerly used by oil burning engines.   *[T. G. Hepburn*

Gresley needed greater engine power on the GE but in 1928 when the first " Sandringhams " were built the engineers still imposed severe limits on axle loading, while the overall wheelbase had to fit a 50 ft turntable. The first 48 engines had the small tender, while Nos. 2800-15 were dual fitted. (The Westinghouse brake pump can be seen in the earlier picture of No. 2800.) No. 2819 *Welbeck Abbey* heads an up express out of Cambridge. [*J. G. Dewing*

SANDRINGHAM CLASS 4-6-0

In 1937 Nos. 2859 and 2870 were streamlined for use on the much publicised " East Anglian " express between London and Norwich. First class maintenance was always a feature of Norwich engines and these two were always in fine condition. No. 2870 *City of London* was on an up Norwich express near Claydon, June 1939, and would return on the 6.30 pm down " East Anglian ". The engine of the up " East Anglian " returned on the 3.30 pm down. Stream-lining was removed in early BR days. [*Dr. Ian C. Allen*

In early grouping days 20 of the Gresley K2 2-6-0s were fitted with Westinghouse brake for use on the GE Section. No. 4688 was recorded near Stratford on a down Clacton excursion made up of GE suburban stock. Like the " Sandringhams " these engines had a bad reputation for rough riding.　　　　　*[J. L. Smith Collection*

GREAT NORTHERN ENGINES

Ivatt C12 Class 4-4-2 tank leaves Parkeston with a Manningtree local in 1936.　There were few engines of the class on the GE in pre-war days, although several worked on various branches in BR days.　　　*[Dr. Ian C. Allen*

No. 8144 was one of 25 engines of LNER Class J19 built between 1916 and 1920 to the design of Hill. They were similar to the ten J18 engines of 1912 but without the ugly leading overhang necessitated by the fitting of tail rods to the cylinders. No. 8144 was at Peterborough East in July 1937.
[*J. P. Mullett*

LARGE

J18 Class 0-6-0 No. 8244 leaves Audley End tunnel with an up freight, 26th June, 1931. Lord Braybrooke, through whose Audley End estate the railway passed, insisted on the construction of ornate portals to the tunnel here and at Littlebury.
[*E. R. Wethersett*

In 1934 Gresley rebuilt a J19 with the same boiler having round topped firebox as that used on the rebuilt Clauds and the following year similar reboilering began on the J18s, which had their frames shortened making them similar in every respect. A former J18, No. 8248 is seen in rebuilt form at March shed, May 1936.
[*H. F. Wheeller*

0-6-0s

One of the impressive Hill J20 0-6-0s built between 1920 and 1922, No. 8282 heads an up coal train near Littlebury, 17th June, 1929. Until the appearance of Bulleid's 0-6-0s on the SR in 1942 these were the most powerful engines of their type in this country. [*E. R. Wethersett*

No. 8185, built in 1901 was rebuilt with Belpaire firebox in 1929 and the unreboilered J16 Class became extinct three years later. No. 8185 was emerging from Littlebury tunnel with an up freight, 17th May, 1930.

[E. R. Wethersett

J17 CLASS 0-6-0

No. 8214 heads an up freight near Cheshunt in 1939. Nos. 8210-39 were built with Belpaire firebox, as was No. 8189, the first GE engine so fitted. All received superheated boilers in LNER days. [C. R. L. Coles

Unusual combination of " Claud ' No. 8821 and 0-6-0 No. 8192 with a freight at Great Chesterford, 18th August, 1930. Several Clauds had been dual fitted in GE days for work on tightly timed fitted freight trains.

[E. R. Wethersett

An 1888-built member of the class, No. 7833 was recorded at Stratford in March 1927 repainted in the GE wartime grey livery. At this time Stratford was still using up old stocks of grey paint on its less important engines. The E4 Class 2-4-0 No. 7473 has received LNER black livery.

[*H. C. Casserley*]

J15 CLASS 0-6-0

No. 7932 was recorded near Barnham on the Bury St. Edmunds-Thetford branch. There were ammunition and poison gas dumps near here and this was one of three Bury J15s fitted with internal type spark arresters on a stovepipe chimney during the Second World War. [*J. G. Dewing*

Second of the class, No. 8001 in grey livery, stands next to one of the engines it replaced, Holden 0-6-0 tank No. 358E, Stratford shed, 12th July, 1924. The '' E '' suffix to the GE number was a temporary arrangement before 7000 was added to provide the new LNER number.   [*J. L. Smith Collection*

No. 8004 enters Enfield Town with a train from Liverpool Street, 1939.   By this time condensing gear had been removed. Nos. 8000-11 had Westinghouse brake only and never left the GE Section.   [*J. G. Dewing*

Five of the 1924 series, Nos. 990/1/6/7/9E, were loaned to Neasden in 1925 for use on special trains between Marylebone and Wembley Stadium for the British Empire Exhibition. At this time Nos. 992-5E were working from Hatfield on Kings Cross locals. These dual fitted engines soon returned to the GE Section. No. 996E is seen near Neasden with an Exhibition special. [*L.P.C.*

One of the Gorton built 1927 engines, No. 2632, approaches Stratford with a Gidea Park local formed of Gresley articulated stock. In latter years nearly all the N7s were fitted with round topped fireboxes. [*J. L. Smith Collection*

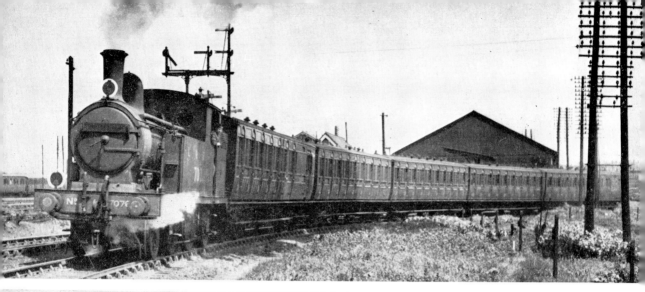

F4 2-4-2 tank No. 7076 on the west curve Stratford with a North Woolwich-Fenchur Street train. [J. L. Smith Collect.

STEAM

F5 Class 2-4-2 tank No. 7785 heads a Lough train up Bethnal Green bank with the later 5 GE suburban stock built 1911-24. Note bar windows, a feature of all GE suburban coach [Dr. Ian C. A

G4 0-4-4 tank No. 8116 pauses at Custom Ho with a train for Becton, 15th July, 19 The train consists of the 27ft six-a-side fo wheelers of 1899-1905 vintage, many of the la examples having been placed on bogie und frames to form 54ft coaches. As four-whee the type disappeared about 1936. [H. F. Whee

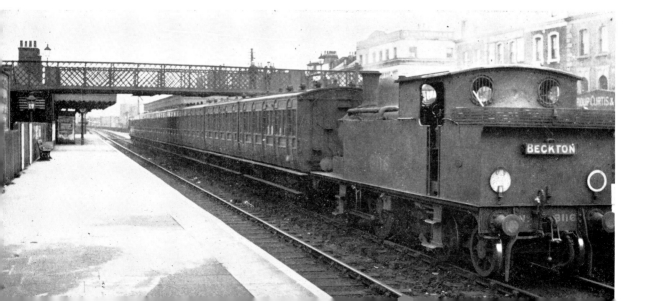

F5 2-4-2 tank No. 7095, still with GE built up chimney, heads an up train of assorted vans out of Stratford. [*J. L. Smith Collection*

SUBURBAN

Holden J67 0-6-0 tank No. 7267 approaches Chingford with a typical "jazz train", 1st June ,1925. [*F. J. Agar*

Holden J69 0-6-0 tank No. 7160 marshals a parcels train in Stratford sidings. The leading vehicle was built in 1910 as a Brake 3rd, but was converted to Ambulance Train use in 1914. After the war it was one of eight such vehicles to return to traffic as a parcels van.
[*J. L. Smith Collection*

In 1914 Hill borrowed the diagrams of the LBSC Westinghouse air controlled motor train gear perfected by L. B. Billinton and a modified form was fitted to small 2-4-2 tank No. 1311 for trial on the Mildenhall branch. In 1915, No. 1304 was similarly fitted and from the 1st March, 1915, the two engines ran motor trains for workmen on the Edmonton-Cheshunt line. The clerestory coaches were of 1904 and 1906 vintage and survived until 1956. [L.P.C.

PUSH AND PULL TRAINS

After the war three more F7 2-4-2 tanks were fitted and they worked the Seven Sisters-Palace Gates service from 1920. No. 8305 was recorded on this duty at Palace Gates in 1937. [J. G. Dewing

Another F7 2-4-2 tank was unique in being fitted in 1924 with the GCR type mechanical push and pull gear, and in this form it operated the Quainton Road-Verney Junction service with a 12-wheeled GCR coach No. 8307 is seen at Quainton Road, September 1935. The service was withdrawn the following year. [J. M. Jarvis

In 1938 two NER G5 0-4-4 tanks were transferred to Stratford to replace the rather feeble F7 tanks. They were used on the Palace Gates' service until it was withdrawn in 1942. The motor trains were reintroduced in 1948, but finally withdrawn in 1951, when the NER 0-4-4 tanks and GE motor train sets, three of each, were transferred to Cambridge for use on the Audley End-Saffron Walden-Bartlow service. In BR days, No. 67322 stands at Bartlow, 25th August, 1956. Two months later the service was taken over by N7 0-6-2 tanks and stock with vacuum controlled motor gear.

[R. C. Riley]

Ex NE 0-4-4 tank No. 67269 propels a GE motor train set near Bartlow, April 1955. The leading coach is of special interest, being one of the GEs first bogie coaches, built for the Cromer service in 1897. Two such coaches were converted for motor train use and they survived until early 1957.

[Dr Ian C. Allen]

In 1922 the GE introduced a simplified form of working on certain rural branches. Existing coaches were converted with a centre gangway and corridors to enable the guard to issue tickets and only the end doors in each coach were available for use. F4 2-4-2 tank No. 7077 was at Braintree, April 1932, with the Bishops Stortford train of conductor guard type coaches. [*Dr. Ian C. Allen*

CONDUCTO

Holden's small J65 0-6-0 tank stands at Eye station, 22nd April, 1930, with a Mellis train, the rear coach of which is adapted for conductor guard working. This three-mile branch with intermediate halt at Yaxley lost its passenger service in 1931. [*W. Potter*

E4 Class 2-4-0 No. 7503 heads a down Mildenhall train near Coldhams Common, 3rd August, 1934. The 1893 vintage stock was converted for conductor guard use 1922-23 and withdrawn by 1940. Latterly bogie coaches were used, one of which was fitted with a retractable step controlled by the train brake for use at halts.
[*E. R. Wethersett*

UARD TRAINS

Basic ingredients of a GE halt—steps, an oil lamp, a name-board and a trespassers warning notice. The young lady has alighted from this Bury St. Edmunds-Thetford train at Seven Hills Halt, May 1953. Four of the five branches on which conductor guard trains were used are illustrated—the fifth was that from Maldon East to Woodham Ferrers. Other GE branches were later similarly worked in LNER days; in recent years BR has revived the idea with diesel multiple unit trains.
[*Dr. Ian C. Allen*

Busy scene at Hunstanton on August Bank Holiday Monday in 1933. From left to right the engines are F3 2-4-2 tank No. 8091, D13 4-4-0 No. 7729 and J15 0-6-0 No. 7552.

[W. Potter

BRANCH LINES

F3 Class 2-4-2 tank leaves the Framlingham branch at Wickham Market Junction with a mixed train, July 1948. These engines were replaced soon after by F6 Class 2-4-2 tanks made redundant by London area electrification.

[Dr. Ian C. Allen

G4 Class 0-4-4 tank No. 8122 leaves Audley End with a train for Saffron Walden, 17th May, 1930. The 40 Holden 0-4-4 tanks, built 1898-1901, put in nearly 30 years' service on the "jazz trains" until replaced by LNER built 0-6-2 tanks after which they were withdrawn or transferred to country sheds. No. 8122 was one of only five of the class to lose its condensing gear. The type became extinct in 1938. The bogie coach of 1901 vintage survived until 1955, the 1899 six-wheeler having been withdrawn in 1935.

[E. R. Wethersett

J15 Class 0-6-0 No. 7643 sets back on to the 4.11 pm through train to Chelmsford at Maldon East, 27th July, 1935. Note the fine station building at right.

[J. L. Smith Collection

J69 Class 0-6-0 tank No. 7081 heads a down train of Cory's coal wagons out of Temple Mills sidings, 18th August, 1928. Built in 1904 as No. 81, this engine is a contemporary of No. 87 now preserved in Clapham Museum. [*F. J. Agar*

SIX-COUPLED TANKS

J66 Class 0-6-0 tank No. 7293 heads an up freight from the docks lines approaching Colchester, 4th August, 1933. [*F. J. Agar*

Y4 Class 0-4-0 tank No. 7227 at Stratford, March 1938, was one of five of the type built to Hill's design, 1913-20. The outside cylinders and Walschaerts valve gear were unusual features on the GE. All were used in the London area. [S. W. Baker

FOUR COUPLED TANKS

The "Coffee Pot", Y5 0-4-0 tank No. 7230 was the last survivor of its class. Built in 1903 it was used as a Stratford Works' shunter until 1948 and often appeared at pre-war exhibitions of rolling stock organised by the LNER. It is seen at such an exhibition at Stratford, 1934. [C. R. L. Coles

F4 Class 2-4-2 tank No. 7072 was one of 16 such engines to be armour plated in 1940 for hauling War Department coastal defence trains. Most of them had the armour removed in 1943, though some survived in this form until 1945. No. 7072 was recorded at Stratford, 22nd May, 1943, on return from loan. [W. Potter

0-4-0 Tank No. 7133, built in 1897, at Wisbech on an Upwell train before the passenger service was withdrawn on 31st December, 1927. The horse boxes are of GN and NE origin, the four-wheeled 1875 brake van was converted for use on the tramway in 1903 and the four-wheeled coaches are two of those built for the Tramway for its opening in 1884.

[*Real Photographs Ltd.*

Four and six-coupled tram engines at Stratford 1946 with side plates and cowcatchers removed. Ten four-coupled trams were built 1883-97, of which No. 7134 was the last built and the last survivor, being withdrawn in 1952. No. 7126 was one of the last of 12 outside cylinder six-coupled trams built 1903-21, all withdrawn by 1955.

[*W. Potter*

TRAM ENGINES

Six-coupled tram in a state of undress —No. 8217 awaits works at Stratford, May 1949. [*H. G. Lawlor*

Two double-ended Sentinels were built in 1930 for use on the Wisbech & Upwell line. Because of high water consumption they proved unsatisfactory and were transferred to Yarmouth for use on the Quay line, where one lasted until 1952.

[*J. L. Smith Collection*

THE
ODD

The Clayton Wagon Co., Lincoln, built 11 geared steam railcars in 1927-8 and several saw service in the Norwich district. They were not particularly successful and all were withdrawn between 1932 and 1937. No. 43305 *Bang Up* was recorded leaving Lowestoft, 30th June, 1936.

[*F. J. Agar*

From 1931 unrebuilt Holden 4-6-0s were transferred to the Great North of Scotland section until by 1942 there were 25 in Scotland. From 1943 some of these were fitted with round topped boilers dimensionally similar to the originals and the decorative valancing above the coupled wheels was removed. No. 1524 was recorded leaving Inverurie, April 1947.

[J. M. Jarvis

J15 0-6-0 No. 7690, built in 1885, was the last Worsdell engine of the class in service.   On withdrawal in 1938 it was sold and ran under its own steam to Gartsherrie Iron Works in Lanarkshire.   Its new owners, Baird & Co. Ltd., owned collieries in the Twechar area before nationalisation and the J15 ran there to collect coal for the coke ovens, by virtue of running powers over former North British Railway lines.   It was overhauled by the Yorkshire Engine Co. in 1952, and looked very distinctive in lined black livery with polished brass dome cover.   Photographed in 1958, it was scrapped two years later.   The Gartsherrie Iron Works did not long survive it, being closed in 1967.   [J. P. Mullett]

The Lauder branch was a light railway opened by the North British Railway in 1901.   Only engines with very light axle load were permitted.   From 1931 GE 2-4-2 tanks of Class F7 were introduced; they were replaced in 1944 by Holden 0-6-0 tanks, allowed to run over the branch with empty side tanks and so permanently coupled to former NBR tenders. Nos. 68492 and 68511 were recorded at Galashiels, 10th July, 1950.   Freight traffic on the branch was withdrawn in 1958.   About 20 GE 0-6-0 tanks worked in Scotland, together with seven 2-4-2 tanks of F4 and F7 classes.

[A. G. Ellis Collection

Electrification of the line from Liverpool Street to Shenfield was first announced in 1936, and to avoid conflicting movements of local and main line trains, work began on the construction of a flyover south of Ilford.   A May 1939 view of work in progress shows " Sandringham " 4-6-0 No. 2802 *Walsingham* on a down express overtaking N7 0-6-2 tank No. 870 on a Shenfield local formed of the GE 1900 train, the brakes being 8-wheeled and the remaining coaches 12-wheeled.

[British Railways

ILFORD FLYOVER

Work ceased during the war and the flyover was not opened until 2nd October, 1947.   No. 1629 *Naworth Castle* heads an up express past new L1 2-6-4 tank No. 9000 posed on the flyover with local train stock, 30th September, 1947.

[British Railways

L1 2-6-4 tank No. 67701 emerges from the bridge under the main line at Stratford Fork Junction, 16th February, 1957, with a North Woolwich-Palace Gates train.
[R. C. Riley

EAST LONDON STEAM

Two J69 0-6-0 tanks pass Shoreditch in charge of a Loughton-Eastbourne Sunday excursion, which they would haul over the East London line as far as New Cross Gate.
[J. J. Smith

East Side, West Side—the two immaculate station pilots stand at Liverpool Street, 11th May, 1957.   [*R. C. Riley*

LIVERPOOL STREET PILOTS

The East Side Pilot made rare forays on the " Jazz Trains " if the West Side Pilot had already been pressed into use. Such was the case on 7th May, 1959, when No. 68619 was recorded near Hackney Downs on the 5.27 pm Liverpool Street-Chingford.   [*K. L. Cook*

Exception to the rule that "Jazz Train" engines normally worked chimney first out of Liverpool Street, 0-6-2 tank No. 69604 approaches the terminus with a train from Chingford, 23rd September, 1958.   [R. C. Riley

JAZZ TRAINS

LNER built N7 0-6-2 tank No. 69665 leaves Liverpool Street on an Enfield Town train, 23rd September, 1958.   In background No. 69634 stands in an engine dock prior to working a Chingford train.   [R. C. Riley

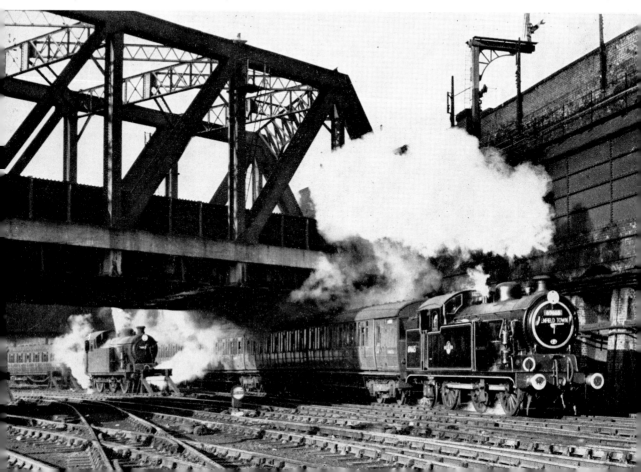

London Transport Central Line trains replaced GE line steam trains to Epping in September 1949, but GE 2-4-2 tanks worked the push and pull trains thence to Ongar for eight more years. F5 2-4-2 tank No. 67200 takes water in Epping station, while working the Ongar service, 14th April, 1957.   [K. L. Cook

ONGAR BRANCH

Another F5 2-4-2 tank, No. 67203, pulls out of Ongar, 18th May, 1957. London Transport electric trains took over the branch working six months later.   [R. C. Riley

WITHAM

" Sandringham " 4-6-0 No. 61655 *Middlesbrough* passes Witham on the 9.30 am Liverpool Street-Harwich, 2nd August, 1958. The Junction signal box was demolished by 1961 to enable the platforms to be lengthened.   [*K. L. Cook*

Thaxted terminus of the 5½ miles branch from Elsenham opened as a light railway in 1913, with J69 0-6-0 tank 68579 and coaches 62450 and 62461 built at Stratford for ambulance train use in the 1914-18 war. Photographed 10th September, 1952, the last passenger train ran three days later and goods traffic was withdrawn from June 1953. Note the small shed to accommodate one engine, a typical feature of GE branches. [S. C. Nash]

ESSEX LIGHT RAILWAYS

Interior of bogie coach No. 60462, built in 1884 for the Wisbech & Upwell Tramway and transferred to the Kelvedon & Tollesbury line in 1928. These tram type coaches had 2ft 9in wheels instead of the usual 3ft 6in and platforms were built correspondingly lower. This coach was restored to original condition as GER No. 8 in 1956 but subsequently broken up. A similar coach, No. 60461, was sold to a film company for use in " The Titfield Thunderbolt ". Note gas lamps. [J. J. Smith

Tollesbury train in the Low Level platform at Kelvedon, 19th September, 1950. Leading vehicle is of the Wisbech & Upwell type, while the two six-wheelers were built in 1896 for the Denver-Stoke Ferry branch and transferred from that line after its passenger service was withdrawn in September 1930. *[I. L. Wright*

J67 0-6-0 tank No. 68616 on Kelvedon train at Tollesbury, 19th September, 1950. Old coach bodies were frequently used to provide accommodation at branch line stations. The Kelvedon & Tollesbury line opened in 1904 and passenger traffic ceased in 1951, after which freight trains continued to run as far as Tiptree until 1962. *[I. L. Wright*

COLCHESTER

E4 2-4-0 No. 62789 heads the 3.44 pm Cambridge train out of Colchester, 13th July, 1957.   [*K. L. Cook*

Rebuilding of Colchester station began in 1939, an important feature being elimination of the sharp curve to permit removal of the speed restriction. Work ceased during the war and was not completed until 1962. At left the platform is being rebuilt to the new alignment. B1 4-6-0 No. 61384 was in charge of a down Harwich freight, October, 1956.

[*Dr. Ian C. Allen*

BRIGHTLINGSEA BRANCH

Branch line maids of all work were the Worsdell J15 0-6-0s. No. 65448 enters Wivenhoe with the 5.45 pm Colchester - Brightlingsea, 17th April, 1949.

[*T. J. Edgington*

Another J15, No. 65468, approaches Wivenhoe with a mixed train from Brightlingsea, May 1956. Opened in 1866 the line skirted the River Colne and was so badly damaged by flooding on 31st January, 1953, that it was closed until 7th December of that year. All traffic was finally withdrawn in June 1964.

[*Dr. Ian C. Allen*

HORSE
AND
HOUND

Owing to petrol rationing a special train was put on for the Suffolk Hunt on 9th February, 1957, to convey horses, hounds and huntsmen from Bury St. Edmunds to Mellis, with a reversal at Haughley. The empty train behind immaculate 4-4-0 No. 62615 is seen leaving Mellis for Elmswell, where it picked up its return journey load. With one exception, Gresley rebuilds of "Super Clauds" retained the ornate splasher framing.

[*Dr. Ian C. Allen*

N7 0-6-2 tank No. 69717 near Broxbourne with an up Hertford train 23rd July, 1955. The leading vehicle is not what it seems for non-bogie passenger stock had long disappeared from London area services. It is an unique vehicle, a hound van converted from an 1891 built six-wheel 3rd in 1912 and withdrawn early in 1956. [*E. R. Wethersett*

1912 built J68 0-6-0 tank No. 68643 prepares to shunt wagons from the incoming train ferry, 5th September, 1950.
[B. Reading

HARWICH

B1 4-6-0 No. 61005 *Bongo* leaves Parkeston Quay with the up " Scandinavian " boat express, 10th September, 1955.
[W. M. J. Jackson

E4 Class 2-4-0 No. 62795 leaves Cambridge with the 11.15 am to Colchester 14th March, 1953. In the bay platform stands another 2-4-0, No. 62794, on station pilot duties.   [*A. G. Ellis Collection*

CAMBRIDGE

In 1951 five LMS type Ivatt Class 2 2-6-0s were allocated to the GE to replace older engines. No. 46466 leaves Cambridge, 22nd June, 1958, with an excursion to Clacton via the Colne Valley line.   [*R. C. Riley*

MARCH

J15 Class 0-6-0 No. 65420 pulls out of the down sidings at March with empties for the fruit traffic, June 1958. This has the medium length E4 chimney fitted to some J15s in BR days. [Dr. Ian C. Allen

Another J15, No. 65474, one of the last of the class built in 1913, starts out of March with a Wisbech train. This type of canopy was once a commonplace feature of GE stations. [T. G. Hepburn

Rebuilt Claud 4-4-0 No. 62610 leaves Ely
with the Hunstanton portion of the 12.24 pm
Liverpool Street-Norwich, 25th June, 1958.
[R. C. Riley

Another rebuilt Claud, No. 62534, approaching Ely with the 2.3 pm from Kings Lynn, via March, 26th April, 1958. The fine GE splitting distant signals for Ely North Junction refer to the lines to Thetford, Kings Lynn and March, in order of importance. This gantry survived until 1963.   [R. C. Riley

An interesting feature of GE signalling was the use of nice little fogman's repeater signals. These were the repeaters for Ely North Junction distants.   [R C. Riley

STOUR VALLEY LINE

E4 2-4-0 No. 62790 pauses at Cavendish with a Cambridge-Colchester train, July 1955.   Note the impressive station house.   [*Dr. Ian C. Allen*

E4 2-4-0 No. 62786 approaches Haverhill with a Colchester-Cambridge train, July 1951, the leading coach being of GC origin.   At right Ivatt 2-6-0 No. 46465, then brand new, which had worked the connecting train off the Colne Valley line, having left Chappel after the E4.   In background Haverhill Junction signal box.

[*Dr. Ian C. Allen*

No. 65391, an 1890 vintage J15, one of five of the class fitted with side window and tender cabs in 1934-5 for tender first working on the Colne Valley line.   It is here seen leaving Cavendish for Cambridge, March 1956.   [*Dr. Ian C. Allen*

Only 13 " Clauds " were not reboilered either as " Super Clauds " or Gresley rebuilds and all survived to come into BR hands. No. 62508 leaving Haughley with an Ipswich-Bury St. Edmunds local, August 1948, survived until 1950 and the class became extinct two years later. The leading coach is of NER origin. [*Dr. Ian C. Allen*

HAUGHLE

One of several 4-6-0s displaced from the London area by the Southend line electrification at the end of 1956, B12/3 Class No. 61576 approaches Haughley with a Bury St. Edmunds-Ipswich local, May 1958. At right the main line to Norwich. [*Dr. Ian C. Allen*

Haughley Junction in 1950 with new K1 2-6-0 No. 62063 on a Whitemoor-Parkeston freight passing J15 0-6-0 No. 65459 on Mid Suffolk Light Railway train.　　[Dr. Ian C. Allen

Haughley station looking north, 23rd July, 1952.　The 10.22 am Ipswich-Bury St. Edmunds is standing on the down main line, while the 11.15 am mixed train to Laxfield stands in the bay with J15 0-6-0 No. 65447 in charge.　The former London suburban bogie coaches replaced the six-wheelers used on Mid Suffolk Light services in October 1951.　The MSLR originally had an independent station at extreme right.　　[R. E. Vincent

MID SUFFOLK LIGHT RAILWAY

Like the Colne Valley & Halstead Railwa in Essex, the Mid Suffolk Light Railwa remained independent until after the 192 grouping, but within a few years both line were almost indistinguishable from an other Great Eastern branch. J15 0-6- No. 65459 tackles the 1 in 43 climb awa from the main line at Haughley with mixed train, January 1950. [Dr. Ian C. Alle

A rake of gas lit six-wheelers at Laxfiel 18th April, 1949. The brake 3rd wa built in 1902, the two composites fiv years earlier. [T. J. Edgingto

Station nameboards on the branch we manufactured locally and quite distincti in pattern. That at Aspall was recorde in June 1952, a month before the tra service was withdrawn. The Mid Suffo Light and the narrow gauge line betwee Halesworth and Southwold provided tl GE with its only competition in Suffol although not of any great significance. [I. L. Wrig

FRAMLINGHAM BRANCH

J15 0-6-0 No. 65389 pauses at Marlesford with the pick-up goods on its way back to Wickham Market, 3rd May, 1958. The coach body is a 3rd brake of 1877 vintage, withdrawn in the first decade of this century. The branch passenger service ceased in 1952, but freight traffic survived until 1965.

[R. C. Riley

Framlingham shed, May 1952, typical of many such sheds at the end of branch lines. It was demolished after withdrawal of the passenger service, but the water tank remained. Coaling was done by hand from a wagon, hence engines with small tenders were the most popular.

[Dr. Ian C. Allen

F6 Class 2-4-2 tank No. 67230 climbs the 1 in 53 grade away from Saxmundham Junction with an Aldeburgh train, December 1955. [*Dr. Ian C. Allen*

ALDEBURGH

Strange visitor to the line was LMS Ivatt 2-6-2 tank No. 41200 loaned from Bangor for the 1949 and 1950 summer services, seen leaving Thorpeness, August 1949. It was said to have been sent from North Wales to Suffolk after an incident involving the Chairman of the Railway Executive during a week-end journey to Aldeburgh to play golf. The branch engine failed and after an hour's delay the relief engine set the golf course alight, much to the annoyance of the members! [*Dr. Ian C. Allen*

J15 0-6-0 No. 65447 stands in the Aldeburgh terminus with the 10.25 am Saxmundham train, 2nd April, 1956. The overall roof was removed before withdrawal of the passenger service in September 1966. [*T. J. Edgington*

Thorpeness Station was opened in July 1914. The nearer coach, a 3rd of 1880, provided the Booking Office, while the Waiting Room was formed from an 1897 1st Class coach. Out of sight is the Stores Shed, which, for variety, had once been an 1883 2nd Class coach! Thorpeness became an unstaffed halt in 1962. [*Dr. Ian C. Allen*

BRANCH

Saxmundham Junction Up Distant on the Aldeburgh branch, a former slotted post signal, still in position in 1968. [*Dr. Ian C. Allen*

Interior of the Waiting Room at Thorpeness. This coach had been one of many suburban four-wheelers widened from 8ft to 9ft to provide increased accommodation. The inset portion can just be detected beneath the notice about conductor guard working. [*Dr. R. V. Coates*

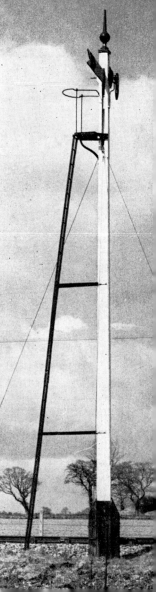

IPSWICH

B12/3 4-6-0 No. 61571 starts the 1 in 120 climb out of Ipswich with the 3.14 pm Yarmouth South Town-Liverpool Street, 22nd May, 1957. This engine took over the train at Ipswich.   [*R. C. Riley*

KINGS LYNN

D16/3 4-4-0 No. 62580, rebuilt from Super Claud,
pulls out of Kings Lynn with the up " Fenman ",
which it would haul as far as Ely, 21st May, 1957.
[K. L. Cook

99

Lowestoft station in 1954 with F4 2-4-2 tank No. 67174 on pilot duty
and F5 2-4-2 tank No. 67218 with a motor train for Yarmouth.
[*Dr. Ian C. Allen*

F4 2-4-2 tank No. 67199 at Beccles with a motor train from Yarmouth
South Town, June 1955.   These engines were fitted with vacuum controlled motor gear in BR days.   [*Dr. Ian C. Allen*

Ex GNR 4-4-2 tank No. 67366 propels a Yarmouth motor train out of Lowestoft, 22nd May, 1957.

[R. C. Riley

—YARMOUTH

Yarmouth train approaching Lowestoft, March 1957, with D16/3 4-4-0 No. 62546 *Claud Hamilton*, deputising for a failed 2-4-2 tank. This engine acquired the LNER type nameplates on withdrawal of the original engine in 1947.

[Dr. Ian C. Allen

THETFORD

Impressive motive power on the 11.30 am Thetford-Swaffham hauled by 2-4-0 No. 62789 and 4-4-0 No. 62559, July 1955. The 2-4-0 was the regular Swaffham branch engine, the 4-4-0 having worked in on the school train. Rather than leave an unattended engine at Thetford it ran to Swaffham in this manner to relieve the crew, the return working to Thetford also being double headed. [Dr. Ian C. Allen

J15 0-6-0 No. 65469 outside Thetford Bridge station with an engineers' train, May 1954, after renewal of the bridge at Barnham. The passenger service between Bury St. Edmunds and Thetford was withdrawn in 1953 and despite the bridge renewal freight traffic ceased seven years later. The Norwich Engineer's saloon had been built as a clerestory six-wheeler in 1901, was lengthened to a bogie coach in 1904 and fitted with elliptical roof three years later. It went into departmental use in 1940. [Dr. Ian C. Allen

J17 0-6-0 No. 65567 leaves Swaffham for Thetford, 31st March, 1962, with the GE Commemorative Steam Tour organised by the RCTS. By this time the last steam engine at Norwich, No. 65567 has since been preserved as LNER No. 1217E in its 1923 superheated form. [Dr. W. J. Naunton

D16/3 4-4-0, No. 62592 crosses Reedham Swing Bridge with a Lowestoft-Norwich train, August 1952.   This engine carries a staff catcher on the tender for use on the M&GN section.   [*Dr. Ian C. Allen*

SWING BRIDGES

"Britannia" 4-6-2 No. 70003 *John Bunyan* crosses Beccles Swing Bridge with an up Yarmouth express, July 1958. Although only 30 years old it was the high cost of maintaining this swing bridge and that at Haddiscoe that caused the closure of the Beccles-Yarmouth South Town section.   [*Dr. Ian C. Allen*

One of ten of the class rebuilt to two cylinder engines, No. 61614 *Castle Hedingham* heads the 12.36 pm Cambridge-Liverpool Street past Hackney Downs, 1st November, 1958. [*R. C. Riley*

SANDRINGHAM 4-6-0s

No longer streamlined, No. 61670 *City of London* leaves Woodbridge with the 7.26 am Yarmouth South Town-Liverpool Street, 10th October, 1956. [*R. C. Riley*

The scene at Yarmouth South Town on Sunday, 1st February, 1953, after the severe flooding which occurred throughout much of the East Coast. No. 61054 had brought in the Saturday 6.33 pm from Liverpool Street and was marooned until the following Wednesday. Train services out of South Town were not resumed until 18th February.

THOMPSON 4-6-0s

B1 4-6-0 No. 61253 brings the Royal Train off the Framlingham branch at Wickham Market Junction, 2nd May, 1956, HRH The Duke of Edinburgh having spent the night at Marlesford during an East Anglian tour. No. 61399 stands ready to haul the train on to Lowestoft.

[Dr. Ian C. Allen

The first " Pacific " to run between London and Norwich on GE metals was SR Bulleid No. 34059 which ran extensive trials in April/May 1949. Two years later three more were loaned for several months pending completion of the delivery of new " Britannias ", three of which were then on loan to the SR. As might be expected GE men had mixed feelings about the Bulleid engines. No. 34057 *Biggin Hill* heads a down Lowestoft express past Snape Junction on the East Suffolk line, June 1951.

[*Dr. Ian C. Allen*]

PACIFICS

GE men were soon at home with the " Britannias " and put up some fine performances with them. No. 70012 *John of Gaunt* climbs Haughley bank with the down " Broadsman ", August 1957.

[*Dr. Ian C. Allen*]

No. 61564 approaches the single line tunnel at Newmarket with the 4.51 pm Ipswich-Cambridge, 3rd May, 1958. Warren Hill signal box controlled the junction of the line to Fordham and Ely and that to Bury St. Edmunds, which diverges to the right in the background. The foreground platform was provided for horse-box traffic.   [R. C. Riley

REBUILT HOLDEN 4-6-0s

No 61575 pulls away from Hockley with the Saturday 12.17 pm Liverpool Street-Southend, 10th November, 1956. The rebuilt Holden engines had a big share of the Southend line traffic until the end of steam on 30th December, 1956. Note the distinctive headcode.   [R. C. Riley

After the Southend line electrification the London engines were transferred to country sheds to replace withdrawn 4-4-0s, while a few D13/3 4-6-0s were condemned also. Here is No. 61575 again with the Saturday 9.50 am Clacton-Leicester express leaving Colchester and heading for Cambridge, via the Stour Valley line, 16th August, 1958.   [K. L. Cook

FREIGHT TRAINS

Rebuilt J19 0-6-0 No. 64674 shunts the thrice weekly goods from County School at Foulsham, November 1957. The branch once ran to Wroxham, but at this time the track between Foulsham and Reepham had been lifted and the freight traffic on this end of the branch was handled by the engine of the Wells-Norwich freight. This line, too, has since been closed, but the track from Reepham was later relaid to a new junction with the M&GN Norwich City-Melton Constable line. [Dr. Ian C. Allen]

Rebuilt J20 0-6-0 No. 64678 shunts a special sugar beet train at Cockfield on the long Melford-Bury St. Edmunds line. [Dr. Ian C. Allen]

A striking sight and sound as Gresley J39 0-6-0 No. 64770 heads an afternoon Harwich-Whitemoor freight on the climb of Haughley bank, May 1951. These engines also handled summer relief and excursion trains on occasions in pre-war days. [Dr. Ian C. Allen]

J17 0-6-0 No. 65502 pulls out of the sidings at Cambridge with a northbound freight, 19th May, 1957. This engine was one of several of the class with the small tenders preferred on branch lines where only hand coaling facilities existed.

[K. L. Cook

A sturdy little J15 0-6-0, No. 65469, pauses at Harleston, on the Waveney Valley line from Tivetshall to Beccles, with the morning freight from Norwich, January 1955.

[Dr Ian C. Allen

The large boilered K3 Class 2-6-0 was first allowed on GE lines in 1936 and subsequently several engines were allocated to GE sheds. No. 61926 approaches Reedham with the 10.15 am Norwich Thorpe-Lowestoft, 21st April, 1954.   [R. E. Vincent

GRESLEY MOGULS

Another K3, No. 61973, approaching Lowestoft with a goods train consisting mainly of fish empties, 9th October, 1956.   [R. C. Riley

On its regular duty from Cambridge, E4 Class 2-4-0, No. 62785, stands in Mildenhall station. It survived until December 1959. [*Dr. W. J. Naunton*

THE LAST " INTERMEDIATE "

Restored to original 1895 condition as GER No. 490 it is loaded on a trailer at Stratford Works for conveyance to Clapham Museum, 10th December, 1960. [*J. G. Dewing*

An Ipswich-Aldeburgh diesel unit passes the 1906 Aveling Porter 0-4-0 tank *Sirapite*, which worked traffic for Richard Garrett's Engineering Works at Leiston, 9th October, 1956. Later replaced by a battery locomotive *Sirapite* is now privately preserved. Although Leiston is still served by freight trains the private siding has now been lifted. [*R. C. Riley*]

TRANSFER SIDINGS

Brush Diesel No. D.5697 heads the freight from Stoke Ferry past the British Sugar Corporation's 1938 Hudswell Clarke 0-6-0 saddle tank *Wissington* which operates the line from Abbey Sidings to the Wissington factory. The line beyond here to Stoke Ferry, which lost its passenger traffic in 1930, was closed in 1965. A small diesel now handles most of the BSC traffic but one of the two steam engines is also used during the sugar beet campaign. [*Dr. Ian C. Allen*

Another Hudswell Clarke, *Peter* of 1929 vintage, heads empties towards Joseph Boam's sand pits at Middleton Towers, June 1958. Waiting to take a loaded train is J69 0-6-0 tank No. 68498. Because there were no run round facilities here and a train shunt was needed to release the engine, this train was always double headed to and from Kings Lynn. The siding is on the Kings Lynn-Dereham branch. [*Dr. Ian C. Allen*